DREAM WORK

DREAM WORK

POEMS

R. BENTZ KIRBY

Mind Harvest Press
COLUMBIA, SC

Copyright © 2018 by R. Bentz Kirby

All rights reserved.

No part of this book may be reproduced in any form or by any electronic or mechanical means, including information storage and retrieval systems, without written permission from the author, except for the use of brief quotations in a book review.

ISBN 978-1-946052-06-3 (ppbk) ; 978-1-946052-07-0 (ebook)

LCCN: 2018941169

Edited by James D. McCallister, jamesdmccallister.com

Cover design by Marc Cardwell, MarcCardwell.com

Interior Photos courtesy Gail Blackman Eubanks

Author Photo courtesy James Scott

For more information:

Mind Harvest Press
COLUMBIA, SC

Mind Harvest Press
PO Box 50552
Columbia SC 29250-0552
www.mindharvestpress.com
www.jamesdmccallister.com

1st Printing, June 2018

Dedicated to my wife, May Kirby.
Without your love I would not be here.

CONTENTS

Introduction ix

PART I
WHEN AWARENESS COMES

Tribute to the Muse 3
The Sunlight 7
Queen Vashti (Esther I) 9
Wistful 11
Bones Dried Up 13
Reincarnation 15
Random Strands 17
Dream Work 21
Drama Dharma Karma 25
Strawberry Shortcake 29
Forty-six, the World is Spinning 31

PART II
VECTORS CONVERGING

Swing Set 35
Flutterby 37
Goldenrods 39
Honda Bullet 41
Trailways 43
Mother's Cars 45
Fairies 49
Stories from 601 51
April Scenes 55
Blue Ridge 57
Boiled Peanuts 59
Tire Sounds 61
Smell 63
Tony's Pizza 65
Vultures 67
The Trip 69
Moonlight Drive 73

Redemption Poem 75

PART III
UNKNOWN SOLUTION

I Am The Poet 79
Vague and General 81
All These Boxes 83
Doors 85
A Glass of Tea 87
My Father's Wake 89
Rain 91
It's My Fault 95
Dreams of Sleep 97
Out of Plumb 101
You Called Me 103
Wind and Water 105
Snowflake 109
Ghost 111
Verdict 113

Acknowledgments 115
About the Author 117

INTRODUCTION

There's a world full of seven billion brains, and the Bentz Kirby I know as my Brother-In-Love wants to know all of them. In this book, I think he's getting started with his own.

Bentz is a journeyman in life. While living predominantly in his adopted hometown of Columbia, SC, he travels regularly to cities in and around the South. From meet-ups of his high-school friends in Georgia, to traveling through the Carolinas and Tennessee to listen to music that drives his soul—and to perform his own songs that may drive others to explore—Bentz is himself a traveler. He has been so since his younger days, first in Easley and Camden, SC, and later Thomasville, Ga., and his college years on a track scholarship at Baptist College (now Charleston Southern University), to his time at the University of South Carolina School of Law. As a lawyer based in Orangeburg, he's driven all over interstates and country roads.

Through all his travels in the physical world, he has also been navigating his dreams, having a conversation with them that continues long after the physical journey has ended. *Dream Work* opens with an Odyssean proclamation for the Muse to sing, moving on to a Penelope-esque image of curled hair, an image of a strong-woman's radiance and beauty kept in the poet's mind for the beginning of this journey. He purveys this image of his lover throughout this book, while concurrently pondering the boundary between life and death, and how love and yearning may or may not exist in the transition between the two states.

Noting this transition, the poet speaks not from some thoughtful position, but from pure experience. While driving on a road trip to Westminster, SC several years ago, Bentz suffered a sudden cardiac arrest. Doctors did not consider the event a heart attack, but the shock to his heart was so much that he lost consciousness while driving through Easley. His wife May (who is present in many of the poems in this book) put the car transmission into park at a Wal-Mart and pulled him out of the car. As Bentz lay on the asphalt parking lot, the remaining air in his lungs expelled and his heart stopped, rendering him clinically dead. Were it not for an off-duty EMT with a defibrillator in her car, Bentz would not have seen this book to publication.

According to him, this event was not a near-death experience. Bentz has stated often that he was gone. The crossing over has informed the revisions to his work before his death, and certainly the work he began after his death.

The poet digs right into this idea of reincarnation early in the book, albeit indirectly, in a poem using that term as its title.

"So, the best I can figure/I am continually reincarnated/yet so much resists change./The same mistakes,/the same insensitive unaware avoiding-intimacy me/is born again, no matter how hard I promise/to be born anew."

That said, this journey is one of redemption, of change, of retooling, of the manifestation of all the knowledge gathered in the years and decades of a musician-lawyer's analysis. *Dream Work* is punctuated with this approach. The images that a musician pulls out, such as in the title poem: "Dreams of children/playing with serpents/on the sandy banks/of newly defiled fields"; "Dreams of walking into/what appears to be a diner/when in fact it is/a coven for dark magic/seeking to strip out/all the light from within…" The lawyer arming an image for full effect, as if to convince a jury: "Moving toward the bus,/reconsidering his earlier decision,/he returns to the newsstand/ to purchase a *Cavalier*./A 10 hour Trailways bus ride/from Georgia into Carolina/through the dark heat/and the humidity adding/ten pounds to his skin/suffocating and reminding him/just who is in control." ("Trailways")

Much like "Trailways," Bentz takes you all over his tramping grounds: on the way to Orangeburg, to Camden, on the way to Georgetown, lowcountry communities along the Sampit River, the Blue Ridge, Atlanta. Moonlight drives down familiar highways: 176, 301, 521 and other unnumbered ones. Cars such as the ever-reliable Honda, and the memories of Galaxie, Buick, Torino, Dodge, Cutlass, Chrysler.

By the culmination of his journey, the poet informs the reader that he is what he always was, a poet, albeit encumbered by work, by the social demands of what he should do in this world to make a buck. The poet isn't cursed, but also isn't enlightened. In the end, the poet is the poet, and the journeys on the roads and in his dreams are his. As he says in "All These Boxes," "Do they know the boxes?/ That they are all mine?/All these boxes?" These dreams and these journeys are indeed the poet's. But gratefully, Bentz has written down these journeys, and they are boxes that are opened up, for us to look over, and maybe consider what our own journeys and dreams may reveal to us.

— Worthy Evans

PART I
WHEN AWARENESS COMES

TRIBUTE TO THE MUSE

These days, emergence from the desert
brings a torrent of words
emanating from me.
Without my will,
without my thought.
it seems they gather slowly,
until released.
I simply record what She would say.

Later, to tell the truth,
I am not confident I wrote.
I am not confident it was me.
I am not confident at all.
Instead I shrink and sigh,
and raise my tribute to Her,
the Muse who makes me sing,
the Muse who lets me ring,
the Muse whose vessel am I.

Oh, I hope I will sail
unharmed by sirens singing.
Oh I hope once she is complete,
She will not destroy me,
or even lay me at Apollo's feet.
No, it is my endeavor,
for less of me, and more of She,
to sing this song to those,
who like me can only wonder,
what wind brings her
and what wind bears her away.

To you oh Muse, I sing.
Your name I know not,
it is unsaid,
but your glory is not done.
It works its way in spirit,
drawing us near it.
I sing, I sing, I sing.

And joy within me rings
while my eyes dare not stare.
Actaeon's stag horns shall not become me,
from Diana's valley would I flee.
Sweetly calling comes the Muse,
I know her not, but welcome her,
to speak thus, and thus,
in words yet hidden from me.

In an oasis we shall gather,
and share our tales
come forth from blather.
The Muse wild and free,
is welcomed here by me.
To sing, to sing, to sing
of her great beauty, grace and wisdom,
to sing of dreams within me.
Dreams I can not touch nor see,
and surely they can not be,
except within her song,
except within her song.

And so I call her, Music.
My tribute I lay,
while my fears I shall allay,
a tribute here portray.
Sing Muse, sing Muse,
proclaim your glory!

THE SUNLIGHT

Watching you
From my back
Is perfect.
Your curled hair,
Afternoon sunlight,
Filtered through blinds and
Splashed around your face.
I see each suspended particle of dust,
Wrapped in golden light,
Framing your freckled face.
Your endeared face,
Your beloved face,
Your loved face.
My mind snaps a photograph.
It will not be enhanced.
It will not be changed.
It will not be forgotten.
It will be beloved,
And retained.
I hold you there,
In wonder.

QUEEN VASHTI (ESTHER I)

She waltzes into the room
exposing my genetic code,
and telling strange and tragic tales
of Vashti and her heroines.

Kindly set my table!

As I recall,
the Son of Mercury said to me.
"It is a sunlit day.
All refuge has been withdrawn.
Your own blood shall whet the stone
to grind your bones.
Until you refuse
to deny
your heartbeat
anymore."

WISTFUL

You may call me wistful,
when I think of your freckled back
and how perfect it seemed to lie next to you
with my honest smile escaping.
You may call me wistful,
when I spend my time in past
and think of how we flowed
together like the water and the earth.
It is obvious I am wasting my time
dreaming of yesterday,
of your smell, of your taste
of your promise and the beauty you invoked in me.
I know I am living in the past
dreaming of the heights
and the exhilarating plunge
into the waterfalls of you.
I am sure you would remind me,
it was me that made the choices,
crushed the flowers,
killed the essence.

Oh, you might call me wistful,
thinking of the way I should be feeling when
your face appears in my mirror,
until all else is eclipsed
by the living memories of our moments,
each one tasting
like the sweetness of your face.
Oh, who would not be wistful,
if like me they had a taste.

BONES DRIED UP

I have been loving you so long girl,
that my bones dried up.
It's like trying to see the world
in the bottom of a paper cup.
Maybe if I was big enough
you could see what I do,
sitting here in the valley.

Oh, I have been loving you so long girl,
that my bones have dried up,
leaving just a shell,
a husk for some amusement,
a trinket for display.
Drill a hole in me,
wear me around your neck.
You can tell everybody,
this was my boyfriend,
before he loved me so much
his bones dried up.
But don't you think
He goes well with this outfit?

What can I say?
I have been loving you so long,
till the marrow is all gone.
Till all the morrow is gone.
Till all is gone.
Till.

REINCARNATION

On the best of days I struggle to understand those
who believe they are reincarnated after death to life again.
For, upon listening to my wife, and others,
I am quite convinced I am reincarnated
at least four times a year.
The same patterns of behavior
occur over some finite period of time.
The discussion of this behavior
usually ends with an affirmation
wherein she has heard the same promise
I will change many times before.

I am continually reincarnated
yet much resists change.
The same mistakes,
the same insensitive unaware avoiding-intimacy me
is born again, no matter how hard I promise
to be born anew.
No matter how hard I promise God
I will change if he will just get this behind me,
no matter how many books I read on analysis,
no matter how many times I write out my goals,
the same old me is born again.

RANDOM STRANDS

Random strands flung across the universe
with varying degrees of success and failure
often return in ways unimaginable to us
but proven to be true.
More true than we recall
with idle memory and
knowledge beyond that
we believe to be encoded within.

A young woman's strand of hair
across her face can implant a vision
in an admirer's mind
which results in dreams
both good and bad
for years to come.
All from a random look
at a finger wiping away a strand and
revealing eyes that speak
to the depth and beyond.
Our romance is a random strand
flung across our universe.

A random thought on the sidewalk
may lead to a random strand
of events leading
to a sequence of random events
leading to a joyous unification of random strands
which seem to be encoded
to dream the same dreams.
A vision suggesting
random strands across the ages
returning to the earth
to be perfected in
a random strand life after life.
You must have the courage
to follow a random strand
which conjures your name.

Random strands of conversation
lead to random decisions
changing the course of your
chosen path for better or worse.
Strands might lead you to a career or lifestyle
you would have eschewed
if you had thought about
that random strand of conversation
thrown across the universe
into your path.

For better or worse,
a random word can emit
from a random thought
from a random strand of events
tracking and hunting you down
until you do not know
what you are doing
or how you emerged there.
Random indeed.

In this life nothing seems
more random than
a moment of time
which may be unknown to others,
which leads two people
further and further away
from the knowledge of
a random strand of DNA
flung across the universe
only to return with the help
of a random computer program
on a random world wide web
of random internet programs
priming the pump for a fee
to tell you what you could never see.

But what could be more joyous
than two random strands
finding their relative bodies
to be related
through unknown circumstances
and illogical results.
Finding random strands through the ether
and across the years
is a random joy
which cannot be denied.
Especially when the details are revealed.

God said go forth and multiply
but he did not mention the consequences,
both wonderful and sad,
which could result,
until a random strand
can appear to confirm
that the void was indeed void
but is no more.
Bless you and your random strand
which was lost and is now found.

DREAM WORK

Within this dream work
live revelations concealed by intention
within unknown
and unfathomed time.
What is to be avoided?

The dreams are elaborate fantasies
created in a human chemistry lab
envisioned and forgotten
as the path is wrought
with danger and unkind memories
demanding acknowledgement.

Why do I resist
the siren call of sleep?
I am avoiding grappling
with the reality of
each waking moment.

Dreams of farmers
tearing down sacred groves
in ignorant attempts to profit
from that which is not theirs
and leaving them unholy in the wake.

Dreams of children
playing with serpents
on the sandy banks
of newly defiled fields
where the Goddess is evicted
by machines ripping her trees and groves
from grounds now fallow and
dominated by lost worship
of all that matters.

Dreams of walking into
what appears to be a diner
when in fact it is
a coven for dark magic
seeking to strip out
all the light from within
and where shadow beings
attempt to seize
those who travel with you
unless you take a hero's stance
and quell this satanic quest.

What are these battles and
why should they endure?

Perhaps it is my unwillingness
to acknowledge that which is,
or to move through passages
fraught with danger and destruction
to obtain the power
to live above the fray
which never ceases
for even one day.

Perhaps it is a lack of courage,
or even a lack of skills
necessary to undertake the journey
to resolve disparate feelings
which reside within,
although they are not my choice
or the result of my actions.

Dream work some nights
leaves me awake
envisioning the ever closing gyre,
where a circle of birds of prey
I do not acknowledge
descends and surrounds me.
I have no idea
what they seek
to sustain themselves.

Dream work is more work
than I am prepared to accomplish.
I wonder why it is so fantastic
observing the perplexing complexity of the construct
surrounding my mind-scape of dreams
unknown and untold.

DRAMA DHARMA KARMA

Dancing on strings controlled
by a puppeteer who handles you
so well you imagine you are capable
to choose who you are
by free will.
You forget the effects of
what you call karma even though
you do not even want to know what it means,
or even if it means anything at all.

You cannot even tell cause and effect
when one of you is acting or dancing
while the string is jerked and
you hop like Punch, or Judy.
Inside, your actions create ruts
full of memories
which cause all other actions
and cause you to believe
that is who you are.

Did you know,
are you aware,
there is no you controlling you,
only the one you choose
to reveal to others?

Drama is kind of clear
when you are in it
or when you see
the attraction to attention
and the choice of prevention
of that convention
controlling what is revealed
with nothing left concealed.

Consciousness is the
result of the application
of the Dharma
to what you realize
and what you create
which perhaps creates karma
which is the complex you create
with all those selves
hiding in the closet of their shameful behavior.

And does that behavior
create your karma
and predict your achievement,
if there is even such a thing?

What is the drama you create?

What is the Dharma which rules it all?

What is the karma you become?

There are many selves
and when awareness comes
you allow the many to dance
throughout the day and night
until you surrender to the eventual.

Drama, dharma, karma,
an unholy trinity for you to acknowledge
but there are other names
and too many games.
Fear keeps you stuck there
when you dance your marionette routine
to the strings which you imagine
guide you in the dance
which should go on forever
within the music of the spheres.
Dance on with your drama,
karma and Dharma.
Forget today.
Forget I even said all this.

STRAWBERRY SHORTCAKE

Sometimes, it seems friendship
cannot last.
To be friends
you have to open doors to what
you do not want others to see.

When a friend sees me,
in my most difficult form,
will they remain
involved at all?
It would be much easier
to withdraw and say,
"Oh, he is just so difficult."
or even,
"Oh well, he used to be nice,
but now he seems to want
more than I can give."

Once in a while,
the worst is revealed.
I know it, regret it.
It troubles me with worry
and honesty surely will drive you away.

But, if you were not my friend,
these sides of me,
you would never see.

So, when you wonder,
"Is he really worth the effort?"
remember,
when the world is closing in,
I will bring you
strawberry shortcake
and sit with you
in the silence of the sun
beneath the trees,
observing the dance
while I listen with you
and the wind of God
will come whispering through our souls
wherever we may be.

FORTY-SIX, THE WORLD IS SPINNING

Lately it seems clearer
the world is spinning,
seemingly slowly, but faster than I imagine.
Food does not taste as good.
And I imagine every possibility,
as if I have become my grandmother.

"I wonder if he washed his hands after
his bathroom break?"
I think while watching the
boy who is scooping up those fries.
Then I even think about the
allowable government standard for
maggots in the meat and the like.

I have noticed when
I talk on the phone
my thoughts seem to
reverberate through my body,
seeking fullness in the ripples
emanating from my self.
It is as if someone
tuned the lens.

I wonder if this has value.
Watching, as if out of body,
I see pictures bubbling up.
I wonder if the world can turn
faster, just for me?
Somehow in this mass, I must
seize my bliss, a kiss, a what?

I have noticed how I talk to my Self
and I do not like it so much anymore.
Something has to change.

The cat jumps down when I sneeze.
There is pleasure in watching
her stretch out on the floor.
Maybe my mind is just fine tuning itself.
Or, I am more aware.

Or, it's only that I am about to turn 46.
Whatever it is,
I know I will have to find
new food to eat,
begin taking my lunch to work.

PART II

VECTORS CONVERGING

SWING SET

Outside Georgetown, Highway 521
separates from US 17-A towards Andrews.
At this point, the road becomes four lanes.
The black swamp bottom suggests
these are wetlands.
I do not mind the fact
two roadside stores will
be taken down for progress.
Yet, my heart has stopped each time,
today the worst.
The swing set is gone.
The house disassembled
dream by dream.
The skeleton remains.
Dreams evicted
from the garden.
No more voluntary ejections
from the swing to see
if one can become gravity free.
Gone dreams dreamed,
plans planned, forts and clubs
with no girls allowed,
or tea times with Pooh.

The shade tree uprooted,
its roots burned in the mass
of vegetation the
paper mill rejected.
Make way, make way,
four lanes are king.
Make way, make way,
azaleas, roses, camellias,
canna lilies all,
make way.

FLUTTERBY

From Sampit, it is about 60 miles
with no town, no community,
only the AME churches dotting the roadside.
Running this road is faster than the
speed traps in small towns where
badgeholders await.

Today, I notice how
the parched corn stands three feet tall
with ears dead on the stalk.
Wondering if these crops are insured,
I spy how tobacco and cotton thrives.
(The climate is perfect for hemp or cannabis).
On a road where grass has retaken
at least a foot on each side,
it is easy to invade reclaimed space
before you notice.

Everywhere, hundreds—no, thousands!
Their wings flutter by,
yellow, red, sulfur,
dancing their dance,
a dalliance with chance.

I have crashed the ball,
not meaning to,
this car violates their dance.
From roadside grass,
to blooms, and crops,
the dance goes on.
Flutter by,
your metamorphosis complete.
Please dance for me.
Please dance for me.

GOLDENRODS

Stark images,
shaved lands stretch outward,
inhumane sentinels stand in rows
reaching forever,
carrying the juice
in cables wired to glass receptacles
and hung on dead trees.
It suggests mechanical worlds
devoid of human touch.

But here,
where butterflies once congested,
the stalks of cotton plants hold
bits and pieces of white
splashed across the fields
where a bale of cotton designed
to fill a tractor trailer
sits covered from the rain.

And all throughout the ditches,
throughout the now fallow fields
which bear traces of the summer's bounty,
the king raises his golden head.

Bright, yellow, top-heavy
bending down to kiss the earth.
And in some fields, it seems
impressionistic brushes have splashed
a blinding golden world refracting
within my brain.

This day the Goldenrod
rules with his scepter
held high against
the used cotton,
against the Carolina sky,
against the road side,
he creeps and fights for his realm.

White splashes add the contrast.
but Goldenrod is King of all.
What gold cannot be spent,
these treasures are held
for those with eyes to see.

HONDA BULLET

From rifled barrel I fly,
spinning through the country
straight down the line,
and faster than time.
The side blurs together
giant cornfield and pines
the vectors converging
on the course I drive.

TRAILWAYS

Moving toward the bus,
reconsidering his earlier decision,
he returns to the newsstand
to purchase a *Cavalier*.
A ten hour Trailways bus ride
from Georgia into Carolina
through the dark heat
and the humidity adding
ten pounds to his skin
suffocating and reminding him
just who is in control.

His mind bounces
between the reality
of the light and the air jet
and whether he can get a seat alone
to pull out the magazine.
(Remember, this is before silicone
and when real women still had a chance.)
At last he gives into his truth
and pulls out the magazine
with its illusory imagination
of impulsive fantasy.

Finally, he rises for the toilet
and thinking, he won't,
he goes in for the finish, the kill
the one to bring forth
the release of a million
wasted possibilities
retained and to be cleaned out in Rome.

On through the oppressive dark
until into Columbia
the bus moves slowly
past the flour towers
past the Sherman stars
past the banks, lawyers,
magazines, papers, dying cinemas,
department stores
and seedy ancient hotels.

Dreaming a Trailways dream,
he has already seen these sights,
but his visions soon disappear
into the haze of a new morning.

MOTHER'S CARS

The other day I was thinking
about my mother and her cars.
The first one I recall was a Ford Fairlane
with three on the column
no power anything,
and no air conditioning.
I remember in 1962
staying up almost all night
helping my father
install safety belts,
because of a television program
about car crashes.
She would not leave for vacation
until she had a seatbelt.
I remember lying on the back deck
watching the stars at night
and the hump.

All her cars, I recall,
had glove compartments,
and when we stopped
at a hamburger stand
she had a table to use
for her food and drink because
she was the Mother.

The next car was a 1961 Galaxie
with an iron dash,
no power anything,
no air conditioning,
no seat belts.
I learned to drive on that car.
It was not easy
turning that steering wheel,
pressing the clutch
and navigating the three on the column.

None of those cars were easy to drive
and all my mother ever talked about
was having a car with air conditioning.

Next my Dad bought her a Buick Station Wagon
with a V-6 engine
and power steering.
I loved that car.
Once I wrecked it
while driving recklessly
on Meridian Road
out by Lake Iamonia
when we were picking up
our tuxedos for the Vashti Prom.
My mother did not like it
because it did not have air conditioning.

What she wanted was a
Ford Torino with power steering
power brakes,
air conditioning,
and a vinyl roof.
Her next car was exactly
that car which lasted her many years.
It was funny seeing her tiny self
in that huge car.
But, it meant I got the Buick
as my car for college.

Eventually the Torino's vinyl roof
faded and began to peel.
Then the air conditioning failed
and she had had enough.
My Dad bought her
a new car from Japan,
a Toyota Cressida,
the best car she ever had.
She crashed it when
her sleep apnea caught up to her
and she sailed off the road into a ditch.

She then had a succession of cars
which were never very nice.
When one died,
my uncle bought a small Dodge
for her which was perfect.
When it died, he bought
her a used Oldsmobile Cutlass.
When it died, my wife
took her to buy a Honda Civic.

But, she did not want a Honda.
She preferred a Chrysler PT Cruiser,
featuring four on the floor
and of course, air conditioning.
That was her last car
because she crashed it
and would not admit it.
She had to stop driving.

What was funny is
if you asked her about the wreck
she would answer, "I never had an accident.
The first time I had one was
Tim's fault cause he told me
to change lanes."
The main thing is,
I remember my Mother's cars
because she never stopped dreaming
of a car with power steering,
power brakes,
four on the floor,
seat belts,
and of course, air conditioning,
until she got it.

FAIRIES

Evening star proclaims itself while
I bow most humble in the presence of such majesty.
The glow behind the darkening trees
suggests another plane of existence
then the picture flickers.

A quantum leap,
a paradigm's shift.

The glow illuminates the glory,
while the trees foretell the coming.

The ancient ones are lurking!
And I, for once, find myself believing
that they live right here.

As I gaze across the open field,
the vast expanse suggests
a greater one within me.

And yet, it seems that if it is true,
how could there be fairies?

Dancing there, within these trees,
as setting sun is feeding magic pots,
and evening star is proclaiming the coming forth
of the King and Queen.

Something here intrigues me,
something here does not seem right.
Would Yeats know these fairies here?
I think not. I think not.

Oh no, the horror setting in,
the ancient ones were here.
Before my kind,
before the Vikings,
before the Caucasian,
fairies danced with their families.

Now, I know the reason,
for the darkening of the trees.
Now, I know the reason,
for the haunting of my dreams.
Now, I know the reason,
we never see their schemes.
These fairies are not ours,
and ours have stayed at
what is left of their home.
It is a longing, longing, longing still,
to give them a home, and I will.

STORIES FROM 601

Heading out across rolling hills
below the fault line
where sand still reigns supreme
and the soil supports
vast quantities of pines,
and fields of cotton
beginning to bloom
with white dots here and there
but still mostly green.

Highway 601 shoots straight across
the midlands out of Orangeburg
into the countryside before your eyes blink.
Past fertilizer bins, cotton gins, and tractors,
and implements stored in sheds with roofs,
mostly rusted quite brown,
or is it red, sort of, though some shine new.

Passing broken wooden fences
and fences mended and white washed
in front of some architect's vision of Tara.
Past a memorial with all three flags
of the Confederacy
and the medical clinic, a small speed trap
called a town and down the hill towards
the ribbon of water we call the Congaree,
where Wateree and Cherokee once hunted
and South below where the great trees
stand sentient over senseless
destruction called progress.

Here, I imagine Sal, Dean and me
in a Rambler, or a Nash, or Studebaker
cannonballing over the driving dipping hills
past weathered grey stores on corners
where no one lives or shops,
or if open, they no longer even sell gas.
Once the lifeblood of this asphalt ribbon,
their rotting hulks stand
telling sad stories of
what once was here,
what the Interstates and Wal-Marts have murdered,
and their ghosts call out, "Revenge me,
take me in, heal my broken spirit."

Yes I see it all as I pass
the coal power poison plant
and the stench of paper bleached
and the consumption of your life blood oxygen.
Why not use hemp instead of pines?

Yes, this road calls out to me,
Highway 601 from Orangeburg to Camden,
and has no happy tales,
only a suffocating sadness
as if to say,
Dean and Sal are dead,
you can go no Further,
there is no Nash, no Rambler, no real cars,
no gas-fueled race through raw Carolina night.
Only greying worn out buildings
hulking and stripped of signs or messages.
The only thing left to do is cry out
for the days when it all seemed possible
and mad, and flowing like that river.

I shout out to them to come and save me,
but the only answer I get
comes from the ghosts of barns,
gas stations
and general stores who cry
such silent tears
along the river of Highway 601.

APRIL SCENES

From a window,
the fading Azaleas drip
pink, red, white, and purple.
On the ground lie their crowns
which make them worth
51 weeks of ugly.

The purple Iris explode,
almost black across the lawn,
just green, so new, uncut,
a promise illuminated by splashes
from the sun.
An impressionist at work.

Meanwhile,
a girl dances on the brick wall
as if she could not resist.
Such primitive joy
untouched by intentions
while her mother sweeps
the concrete floor
of the carport beside the American flag.

Down the street,
a young boy,
dungarees slung below his hips
strikes a beat pose
to impress me
while he drinks a coke.

So gone, so gone.
Once you calculate,
the freedom is gone.

Oh, the Lilies have pushed
up their green pencil stalks
and promise orange, white and red
to come in months ahead.
This vast organism
pulses with the source
until organized, it presses on
against inertia, against entropy,
against matter, against stagnant pools.

Oh sing of the glory,
sing of the glory
April scenes from my window.
A drive-by glimpse
of the wheel which is turning.

Promises, promises
made every year.
April makes them possible.
Like the barechested boy
chasing the calf,
in the newly turned fields,
among the blossoming trees,
I drive on.

BLUE RIDGE

My dream returns to me,
unfolding like a stranger's history.
The Blue Ridge looms on the horizon
after ten hours of driving.
The mountain air, clean, fresh, cold.

In the morning, before scrambled eggs, grits and toast,
I walked into the communal bath,
where I first saw a man with an electric shaver,
and Williams Lectra Shave,
buzzing himself twice a day.

During the day we bathed
in cold mountain water pool,
and walked on rocks in streams,
finding crayfish, lizards and frogs.
Looking for snakes.
The swings and see saw were off to the left
of the front porch with its grand columns.

Beside the playground
was the craft room,
where we braided lanyards and
sewed leather coin pouches
adorned with mountain flowers.
Once I painted a dogwood blossom
on a ceramic tile.

I did not understand why my mother
wanted to sit on the porch,
in those rocking chairs
and look out over the valley for hours at a time.

Now, this has become my desire,
so, until I awake, I rock gently to and fro,
watching birds fly home,
hearing the hoot of the owl,
and seeing the lights slowly flicker out below.

BOILED PEANUTS

At the intersection of 176 and 301
in Paxville, there is a country store
with watermelon aisles and concrete floors,
butt roast, chitterlings and other delicacies
like boiled peanuts.
The legume is pressure heated
over gas burners in salted water.
Drained and bagged for $1.50.
Salty. The new crop are
squishy, almost melting.
The older firm like cardboard are
not for everyone.
My children delight
when the peanuts appear from
the greasy, wrinkled bag upon my return.
More desired than toys,
the pods are strewn across
the room leading to a cross mother.

TIRE SOUNDS

Outside a store,
on Gervais Street at 5:20 PM
it's a Tuesday
and I notice a small detail
the *whiiirrrrrr* sound
tires make as the weight
of the vehicles presses
treads against
the asphalt and rock.
It sounds like a stream
drowning out the sounds,
even the engines,
until it is all one great
ROAR in my ears.
I see the reflections
off the chrome
and the spinners
with the illusion of moving backwards.

Sometimes when I sit
in my car and another one moves,
I feel like I am rolling.
I have to press the brake to make sure.

We are all connected
because I can feel your glare at the signal
and turn to catch your look,
but you are only staring through me
to allow your mind a respite.

On the top of this rise,
glancing back down the street
past the gas station and car wash
and houses rented
to college students,
and the office suites,
furniture stores and UMC church,
my gaze fixates on the western
skyline with the sun
blasting holes through banks
of fading clouds
and highlighting a striking view
of 1970s to present day architecture.
The symbol of man's feeble attempts
to pretend he has power,
the graceful curve of the new dome
counterpoint to the box of the old.
This moment lingers
in the midst of poison fumes
and the roaring *whiiirrrrring* sound
of treads rolling beneath
tons of the folly of man.

SMELL

Walking to the car,
I smell the red clay dirt
Dug next to the parking lot.
For a moment,
I am four years old,
Digging under the floor
Of new construction
With my yellow toy shovel.

TONY'S PIZZA

In the air, voices drift by.
"She called at 2:30, but I left at 2:00."
"We've been here about three quarters of a pitcher."
"No, we don't take checks."

A couple discusses their day.
Two men drink beer,
a softball girl,
tall boy,
"You forgot one of my sandwiches."

With the floor a mishmash
of inlaid splintered brick
the uncovered walls
reflect harsh sounds.

Smoke drifting,
making me wonder
why he thinks he can do that to me.
I would leave,
but I've already paid.

In my mind, there are two worlds here.
They come and go with no concern,
I am watching each one.
When I look, I see.
If I focus too hard,
it draws their attention.

Furtive, I shift my gaze
from the street to the counter
to the wall to the table,
take off my glasses
rub my temples
and begin again
looking out at the traffic.

Something is so clear,
as if I just keep looking
it will be revealed.

While they are flowing on,
it occurs to me that
I am crippled
at the point where
intersections become crucial.

This storm inside
blows bending trees
shattering oaks
twisting trailers
while I am clutching
with my throat constricting.

No one plays the juke box,
waiting on pizza
watching trucks
with our trees
on the way to paper mills.

VULTURES

Sophisticated elegance
of roadside dining is lost upon you,
unless you explore the collective behavior
of turkey buzzards.

In their tuxedos
they await the proper turn
to peck a carrion left by man.
A dog, opossum, raccoon, or deer,
is shared by the clan with dignity
and intelligence.
Some serve, some wait,
but in due time, all will share.

Curious to me that these
large slow birds,
never seem to join their meal.
Hard-pressed, they do not leave the table
until your vehicle is upon them.
Then they circle quickly,
like children playing musical chairs,
to rejoin the meal.

More regal than we care to think,
intelligence and black tie grace,
roadside dining at its best.
The cultured vulture circles round.
Draw up your own chair.

THE TRIP

It is all a haze now,
the memories acid-washed
with trails of intentions
and less than an ounce of prevention.
There was a pattern to our actions
which will reveal itself in time and space
and moving sidewalks
which slip into the future.
Leaving home in a micro bus
and headed to the ATL
where we got lost in rush hour
trying to find the park
to camp in the van.
It began there
with some getting larger
and some much much smaller
than it seemed could be.
The morning dawned
all Kosmic as if a Carnival
had come to town.

At the flying saucer
ready to take off into space
which was only a drop or two away.
Microdots gave way to
Screaming Yellow Zonkers
which gave way to the Devil
wearing an usher's uniform.
It was real, not an illusion.

Three of us had made the journey
on the pilgrimage route to
seek the magic of the alchemist
made up in a laboratory which
is where alchemists work.
The difficulty is communicating to you
what was seen and heard that day.
It is etched in my brain and soul
with John Barleycorn who did die,
along with the Brain Police,
a white bird in a golden cage,
the GA blues and a raging queen.

The next day was to be a free replay
in the park, but
we were off into the ether
lost and not knowing where
this trip was going, except through
the piles and piles of giant snakes
blocking US 19.
But, when the next day dawns
and the darkness bids goodbye
we were home,
only much worse for the wear.

Traveling back is easy
but hard to recall
the days which undulate
out before and behind us
because neither time nor space
can contain the dimensions
of this journey.
Steve Winwood is a God
and we bow in reverence to what
we do not know.

The Trip began with
a tiny step into the future.

MOONLIGHT DRIVE

In the first December chill
limbs of Pecan, Sweet Gum,
Oak and Hickory trees
stretch bare and naked
to grasp the moon
with bony naked fingers.
A peach orchard
raises praise hands to the sky.

At last, the hillside breaks
into the valley.
As I drive the span,
and chase her
across the water,
The Solstice ghost
declares growth is dead,
winter is here.

The cycle completes in death.

It races on, out of reach,
but disappears on spits of land,
to dapple again on water.
Till up the hill,
into the Pine forest whose
silhouette changes not for Solstice.

This Moon shall not return
within my life.
Never shall this ghost
dance so well for me.
It is birth and death alike,
and the bony fingers
have no choice but to stretch,
grasping for that which
lies beyond their reach.

REDEMPTION POEM

Traveling through
my little town
circa 1963-66
on the bypass and
listening to a football game,
an angel touched me
in an inappropriate way.

October 27, 2012 was a day
unlike any other day for me
and my wife, and my daughters
and my family reunion
and my brother's ashes
and my guitar
which never got to play
Black Muddy River.

A dizzy swimming feeling
sinking within growing darkness
into the primal source of being
in which an ineffable essence
combines all into one
and darkness again becomes light.

Into the decision room
where all is accomplished
and all is written into books
for no one to read, I find
it is only the writing that matters.
Down into this disappearing
consciousness where
the illusion of my life
disappears and the veil is
lifted from my eyes.

Down here is where
I find my redemption,
and here I write,
the poem to tell
the story of the veil
which cloaks us all
in darkness.
We can never see
until it becomes
much, much too clear.
The redemption
comes in living
and forgiving
and helping
the lonely soul
who feels like you.

This is my Redemption Poem.

PART III

UNKNOWN SOLUTION

I AM THE POET

I am the poet.
It is not a gift,
nor is it a talent,
rather it is a way of life,
forced down upon me against my will.

Though I should have deserted long ago,
I am clambering, still,
into the silence, into the distance.
Words emerging out of darkness,
into life from energy
like exploding Novas.

Big bang,
expanding galaxy.
From my hair, from my head,
the magnetic belts extend,
shooting energy into the abyss.
Firing only to miss.
This energy is my gift,
my weight, my love, my life,
my death and my organism.

Can you see it? The aura.
The poetic aura?
What of laboring in the vineyard?
I would give all my soul for one line
that clearly defines the happening
at the instant.

I am the Poet.
(I did not say accomplished, or good,
just, that I am.)
Maybe you think it arrogant,
to thus proclaim,
but it is not me,
simply what I see.

Can you see it?
The energy,
the power from around my head?
Can you feel it?
The energy,
transfigured into words,
to bits of information
for interpretation.

If I hint at it.
If I glimpse at it.
If I try to tell you,
then I am the Poet.

Around my head,
around my head,
around my head!
The dance begins,
from nothing into nothing.

VAGUE AND GENERAL

I started with a vague and general sense of purpose
and from there it seems that I have
descended into what appears
to be a morass of mostly
good intentions never
borne to fruition
despite my
best intentions.
I would suggest
that you conduct your
life in a fashion that is more
becoming to your station and manner
and consistent with your birthright and the purpose
granted to you from the one who is when there was nothing.

ALL THESE BOXES

These boxes which once held shoes
are now kept in my closet
and no one but me knows
how they make my life convenient.
As with Pandora
they contain it all just so.

Some shall remain forever closed
for their memories threaten
to hold me, and bind me to
what has past in space and time.

Others await
the most convenient time
to be shared with friends.
Some, I choose to hide
and hope no one looks inside.

Do they know the boxes?
That they are all mine?
All these boxes?

DOORS

Doors can be problematic
although I seldom think
about them or their purpose.

Once upon a time, for instance,
I got stuck in a room with four doors.
With no other way out,
I had to choose.

Though I thought
of walking up to one door,
old with flaking paint
and a real crystal door knob,
I was afraid to try to open
the door without reason.

So instead I refused,
finding myself cast out
from the room
into an inscrutable mystery.

Another day, I came upon two doors
and wanted to open both of them
but they were locked
and I lacked the key.

Another day, I came upon four doors
in a room I could not leave,
and I wondered how
I could open these doors.
It seemed very important at the time.

Then when the Others asked me
I reached into my pocket
and I had many keys
and opened every door
which needed to be opened.

Keep in mind,
these are all different doors
and different rooms
and some require choices
and some you want to choose.

There are Doors of Perception
and doors to keep out the snow
and doors to the astral plane
and doors of a distant journey.
But this one time,
I had the key
to all the doors.

A GLASS OF TEA

Light in October
has the correct angle
to illuminate the essence
of the soul.

Leaves scattered among tables
beneath branches shorn
without clothes
and bleak against
the blue reminding me
of the first time
the sky was truly seen.

Across the uneven bricks
are forms accepting, ordering
moving, connecting, separating
consuming, digesting,
in this time of harvest
where we reap.

On a table is a glass of tea
which somehow seems perfect
and the lemon floats among
the ice cubes huddled together
at the top with a
straw thrust down to
the undercurrents.

As the straw moves all is reflected
darker, lighter, clearer
golden, brown, and just then
a silver reflection of a fork
across the glass.

A tree limb is tossed by wind
and its branches like fingers
are reflected bouncing
through the glass and gone.

Across the table, a friend's
glass sits dull, dark
as if the light prefers her.

For some reason
I cannot pull away
and thinking she must
feel uncomfortable from my stares,
I watch reflections and refractions
from the shadow light.

Across from me
reflected from my glow
is an autumn gift
of rare uncompromising value
reflecting perfect light
from the cave
and places where
the archetypes inhabit my soul.

MY FATHER'S WAKE

My father's wake
is created by a prop
much larger than he
comprehends and a legacy
unknown to him.
Years of difficulty, his
sullen disposition
withdrawing into spaces
I will never occupy or know
except that which lives
within me despite my
best intentions and desires.

Having spent years surfing
in his wake while unaware
of the effect and ripples
which have threatened to
overwhelm me at times,
I begrudgingly allow
the growth of new ideas
and possibilities and new times.

Time moving on informs me
of the need to escape this wake
and all it entails
in order that I might
undertake a new view.

RAIN

The rain defies regulation and resists manipulation
from silver iodide, potassium iodide and dry ice
by men who believe they can subjugate
Gaia, our mother, and bend her to our will.

Recently rain has employed its own rhyme and reason
to this usually dry season, as if to say,
"your computer modules cannot predict me"
as records fall day after day.

Flooding all the areas which
once were swamps and shall be again soon,
the rain reminds us of the futility
of channelling streams underground
without the swamp waiting to receive
the otherwise life-giving bounty
the mother pours upon us.

Destructive, life giving, absent, and overly present
the rain pours as it wills
and not according to your prayers.

Prayer cannot subjugate the rain, it is true.
When my garden is blooming
I love this rain,
unlike when its absence
allows the sun to bake me dry
or overwhelm the ground
until the roots wither and rot.

Read an almanac for a prediction of the unpredictable.
Deal with your space as it was dealt to you
but the rain has no care for you
or your drains or your yard refuse
which dams the rain to pour beyond the sandbags
into your house, store, office, drug store,
warehouse or any other modern cave.

Ignore the power of Gaia at your own peril
believing you are in control with your foolish risks.
But, let us rush on and fill in all the space
made for the rain to live within.
A student dorm and shopping center
can make folks some pretend wealth
which cannot be spent where it matters.

The proof there is no God is the fact
he supposedly gave us dominion
over the earth and all that is within.
Instead of loving care, we murder, rape,
plunder and destroy all there is.

I sit upon the bank of the rivers
and weep over the ignorance which guides us
until the rain one day shall rise up
and show Miami, Savannah, Charleston,
the Outer Banks, the Chesapeake Bay,
Boston, New York and all between
what she has in store.

Today the rain falls and falls until tomorrow
when she deserts us in our desert.
To think, what could be,
If only we had hope.

IT'S MY FAULT

At the risk of
the accusation of egoism
I will accept responsibility
for this goddamn mess
we are in.

First I admit that
I spent too much time
binge watching
what in the old days
they called speculative fiction
so my point of view is skewed.

There is a disturbance
in the force
and the trajectory of our
future has been skewed
to this alternative world
where logic and truth
are frowned upon
and fake news
has more power
than actual news.

Clearly there is only
one answer to this
alternative world
and it is that I do
not belong here.

I was dead, gone
and such was decreed
by the computation
of the universe.
Still, for selfish reasons
I refused to go
and thus the entire
timeline of your existence
has wobbled on its axis.
The future was altered.

And, that is my fault.

Not sure what
can be done now,
but let it be a lesson to you.
The dead stay dead
and save the rest from
the illogical insane reality
we call life.

Yes, it really is all my fault.

DREAMS OF SLEEP

Half-formed ideas
without structure or definition
crowd out the dream of sleep
and race right along
carrying me with them.

Perhaps a digital stimulus
would allow escape
but would not subdue
the forces of nature at work.

Dreams resound with memories
of things past and present,
which obviate the call of dreams
and relegate sleep to a suppressed desire.

Memories pour into the vacant spaces
with no rhyme or reason
and with no structure to be resolved.
Perhaps some new intelligence
is required to wrestle this
into an acceptable state.

Broken promises, broken memories,
broken dreams and broken ideals
litter the pathway,
demanding focus
within the swirling black hole
of every legitimate worry
that the daylight brings.

What is the cure?
Analysis will not allow resolution
and behavior is so fixed
it is not easily revised
to allow some other view.

Know only that my race
to escape that which is me
and my littered pathway
does not allow me
to realize these dreams of sleep.

Instead, some unknown solution
is suggested
although it evades intellect or logic.
Examination of this flotsam and jetsam
offers no logical resolution
for the calcification and plaque
obscuring and obstructing the forms
beyond this dream reality we agree to share.

There is no bypass,
there is no double bypass,
there is no triple bypass,
there is no quadruple bypass,
and there is no quintuple bypass
of these dreams of sleep.

These dreams of sleep
gallop along, untamed
and unfettered
with no objective
but to run yet never be free.

This situation shall require
more study until
the pathway to sleep
is more than just a dream
of a peaceful slumber
where all ideas and feelings
can meet in frank discussion.

OUT OF PLUMB

For some time, it occurred to me
your house is out of plumb.
At the time, it failed to impress me
until the consequences became too significant.

A pearl dropped on your floor
rolls into a corner gathering dust,
cobwebs and other contemptuous qualities
foreign to its nature.

The irony is so rich it would be humorous
under other circumstances
for me to think of intimacy
which has nothing to do with lovers or sex,
but only with friendship.

Whatever runs this place
is deeper than your control,
yet, you deny it.
You fear joy, the path to abundant life,
and embrace the path of danger.

As for me, I have surrendered
my Jesus complex
and my need to save you,
although, like addiction,
wondering if he is your lover
could cause a relapse.

What inventories do you take?
I admit my sickness—I do, I do, I do.
Did I really believe you would love me
if I let you hurt me enough?

You embrace living your problem
with such enthusiasm
it arouses my sadness
springing from your
condemnation of yourself.

Just keep moving,
and if you never stop
you will never have to fall into
the emptiness of you within you.
I do not want to be your lover,
(although sex is not out of the question),
I will use you, let me be honest.
Still, God forbid you might actually feel
what you want.

I have always known
your house was out of plumb.
I lied and told myself it did not matter.
Now I see it has great consequences,
at least for me,
in this dusty cobwebbed place
I do not wish to stay.

YOU CALLED ME

You called me, but I do not know why!

Out of the deep, why not let me perish?

Eased my suffering,
but I have been through hell.
Comforted my losses,
which did not have to happen.
You dressed my wounds,
why not leave me to die?
Put me upright,
when I desired to lay down.
And lit my way,
when I did not want to see.

You called me,
and I wait.
You called me,
and I answered.
You called me,
and I denied you.
You called me,
and I desired you.
You called me,
and I rejected you.
You called me,
and I thirsted.
You called me,
and I drank.
You called me,
and I responded.

Oh wake within me that spirit,
that would walk upon the path
To which you called me.

For when I was weary—you gave me rest.
When I was angry—you softened me.
When I was sad—you comforted me.
When I was depressed—you lifted me.
When I was happy—you danced within.
When I sang—you felt my joy.
When I was lost—you guided me.
When I was stuck—you released me.

Thank you, who called to me
When I did not wish to go.

WIND AND WATER

Wind and Water
are on my mind
these days for a
number of reasons.
It is easy to see
why a storm
brings these elements
to my mind,
but harder to understand
the impact.

One child is in the path
and refuses to leave.
The other is outside the path
and she loses to the
wind and water.

It is inside the house,
inside the cars,
underneath the carpet,
buckling the wood floor,
feeding mold behind
the sheetrock which
must be torn out.

While watching, it seemed
the storm was not a problem.
It did not come ashore and never
hit with the full force which was
possible. But, we still failed to
understand its power.

The cold air met the cold air
and brought the water out of the sea
into the sky and onto the earth,
and into the streams,
and into the rivers,
and into the houses.

The wind from the Northeast
held in the high tide
and left no place
for the water to go
except into homes,
and stores,
and cars,
and trucks,
and motorcycles
and everything.

Waves smashing piers
and undermining all the sand
and dunes and houses built on sand.
Fires erupt running wild
because there was too much
wind to resist the allure of the flames.
Homes gone,
lives gone,
dreams gone, and
life gone
to the wind and water.

Still, the water comes down
from the hills,
and into storm drains,
and swamps,
and fields,
and parking lots
and everywhere
man has covered up the earth.

Still, I wonder why these storms
have such anger,
such sadness?
One can only wish
a lesson could be learned,
but we are too far gone,
and the wind and the water
will wash us all away.

The Wind and the Water
shall remain
with the cockroaches
and they will dance on our graves.
Until the next water,
until the next wind.

SNOWFLAKE

An empty house,
three children gone.
My self, my wife, the cat.
Alone.
Curious, that she seems
to miss the feet and hands
that sent her under couches,
into closets, under tables
and on top of chairs.
Those harassing hands,
that convey love yet.
This pet endowed with love,
seems lonely.
She leaps into my lap.
and we will commune
for minutes,
before sleep.

GHOST

I am certain you are there,
When I turn my head to look
Over my left shoulder
I can feel your breath
In my hair, just there.
I am not sure why
You only appear when we
Are in the car,
But you do.

And I remember when I was
Taking that Christian meditation class
And the leader told us to think of
A bottle floating down the stream
With a note from Jesus.
I asked him why you were there
In the picture, like the meditation was yours.
He said, "There is a reason.
If you saw her, there is a reason."
And that was before you were a ghost.

Sometimes, when I am in bed,
Late at night, I think of you.
But, you are not there.
You are only there
when I am in the car,
And I turn my head just so to the left,
I always feel your breath on my hair
while I wonder where your cemetery
might be—but not your grave.

You are not haunting me.
I only wish I could see,
What you would have me see.

VERDICT

It was not so much that you left,
or even in the way.
It was more in myself,
something you caused me to believe.
Some realm of magic,
formerly out of reach,
felt possible to grasp.
Some distant yearning
that seemed to emanate
from my being,
like a splash across the universe,
like finding my best friend.

And then,
then,
you were just not there.

It would not be false
to accuse you of selfishness.
It would not be false
to accuse you of betrayal.
It would not be false
to accuse you of self-destruction.

Still, those accusations,
though a true bill of indictment,
ring hollow within.
Convicted in absentia,
is no bother to you.
In fact, you disdain the jurisdiction.
No, the trial gives no fulfillment.
It is the aching longing still,
for the vision birthed,
and ended too quick.
You simply changed your mind,
or so you said.

My verdict cannot resurrect me,
nor rekindle the joy
of love the gods have given,
only to remind me
how human I am.

ACKNOWLEDGMENTS

My greatest acknowledgment is to my wife, May Kirby, because without her I actually would not be alive. She is ingrained in everything I accomplish. Additional thanks go out to James D. McCallister and Mind Harvest Press, Marc Cardwell, and Gail Blackman Eubanks who made this publication possible. It is impossible to acknowledge everyone who has supported this endeavor in one way or another, but I'll try. Thanks to Lynn Stowers, James Scott, Marv Ward, Worthy B. Evans, Jenn McCallister, John Starino, Al Black, Cindi Boiter, Bonnie Goldberg, Cassie Premo Steele, Bill Florian and Mariane Parrish for their encouragement and for supporting the arts, and Stephanie Bridgers of the Local Buzz community coffee shop for providing us with an office away from home. A great debt is owed to my late mother, Justice Kirby the librarian, who encouraged reading and thinking in everyone she touched.

Thank you for reading.

ABOUT THE AUTHOR

Bentz Kirby lives in the Rosewood area of Columbia, South Carolina. Educated first as a social worker and later a lawyer, he has been writing poetry since around 1969, but *Dream Work* is his first poetry collection. As a songwriter, he has published two albums of music, *Name Checkin'* with Alien Carnival (2008) and *Secret World* with Jellyroll & Delicious Dish (2017). A survivor of a Sudden Cardiac Arrest, he is a big fan of Automated External Defibrillators. Other than enjoying life with his wife May, their children and a brood of pets, he writes and performs music with his friends.

www.ingramcontent.com/pod-product-compliance
Lightning Source LLC
Chambersburg PA
CBHW021442080526
44588CB00009B/643